Crypto Taxes, Regulations & Legal Basics

Stay Compliant, Avoid Penalties, and Understand Global Tax Rules on Crypto

By Joe Correa

Published by Live Stronger Faster

This book is for educational and informational purposes only. The author and publisher are not engaged in rendering legal, financial, or other professional advice. Readers should consult a qualified professional before making any financial decisions.

First Edition

Table of Contents

Introduction

Cryptocurrency may be decentralized, borderless, and digital, but it is *not* immune to taxation or regulation. As crypto adoption grows and billions of dollars shift into this new financial system, governments around the world are tightening their grip. They want their share — and they're getting smarter, faster, and more aggressive about collecting it.

This book is your essential guide to staying compliant, legally safe, and financially protected as a crypto investor or entrepreneur. Whether you're buying Bitcoin for the first time, trading altcoins daily, staking tokens for passive income, or building a Web3 startup — taxes will touch your crypto journey. And depending on your country, those taxes can be minimal… or absolutely crushing.

We'll start by demystifying how cryptocurrency is classified for tax purposes — because it's *not* just one thing. It can be property, income, capital gains, or even a barter transaction, depending on the context. Then, we'll explore the tax implications of different activities: trading, HODLing, mining, staking, lending, NFTs, and more.

You'll learn about essential reporting obligations — like filing IRS Form 8949 in the U.S., or equivalent documents abroad — and the risks of not doing so. We'll also unpack what to do if you've already made mistakes: missed reporting, lost wallets, or unclaimed income. There's still hope, but time matters.

Next, we'll break down the top tax-friendly (and tax-hostile) countries for crypto investors and digital nomads. Whether you're relocating, setting up a DAO, or launching a token, jurisdiction can make or break your success. We'll explain which countries offer 0% capital gains, crypto visas, and progressive blockchain laws — and which ones to avoid if you value privacy and profit.

Finally, we'll explore the emerging legal frameworks shaping the future: KYC/AML compliance, CBDCs, DeFi regulation, and securities laws that could turn your favorite tokens into liabilities.

This book will not only protect you from tax trouble — it will empower you to *strategically* use tax rules to your advantage. With the right structure and foresight, you can minimize taxes legally, operate globally, and keep more of what you earn.

Welcome to the legal side of crypto. Let's demystify it together — and turn your knowledge into power, safety, and long-term wealth.

Chapter 1: How Cryptocurrency Is Classified for Tax Purposes

Cryptocurrency may feel like digital cash, but from a tax perspective, it's anything but. In most jurisdictions, crypto is not considered currency—it's classified as *property*, *asset*, or even *income*, depending on how it's used. Understanding these classifications is foundational to staying compliant and avoiding penalties. Let's explore how various countries approach crypto taxation and what it means for your personal and business use of digital assets.

In the United States, for example, the Internal Revenue Service (IRS) classifies cryptocurrency as property. This means that buying, selling, or trading crypto triggers a capital gains event, similar to selling stocks. If you hold Bitcoin and sell it for a profit, you must report that gain. Conversely, if you sell at a loss, you may deduct that loss to offset gains elsewhere. This creates a taxable event every time you use crypto—even for something as small as buying a cup of coffee.

But that's not the only classification. If you receive crypto as payment for services (e.g., freelance work, business sales), it's treated as *income*, taxed at your regular income tax rate. If you mine crypto, the fair market value of the coins on the day you receive them is considered ordinary income. Similarly, staking rewards, airdrops, and DeFi yields are all generally taxed as income—sometimes even before you convert them into fiat.

Things become more complex when you start using decentralized applications (dApps), NFTs, or participate in liquidity pools. In many cases, these actions result in taxable events even if you haven't "cashed out." For example, swapping one token for another—like ETH to DAI—is a disposition and a gain/loss must be calculated. Even if you don't withdraw funds, if your crypto earns interest or rewards, the IRS wants to know.

Other countries take different approaches. Germany, for example, treats crypto as private money and allows tax-free sales after a one-year holding period. Portugal currently has no capital gains tax on individual crypto profits. Meanwhile, India imposes a flat 30% tax on all crypto gains, without allowing loss offsets. These variances mean where you live—or *where your tax residency is established*—has enormous impact.

Tax classification also affects how you track your crypto transactions. In property-based systems, you need to record the cost basis, holding period, and fair market value of every transaction. This can be a nightmare without automated crypto tax software. Tools like CoinTracking, Koinly, and TokenTax help streamline this process, importing transactions from wallets and exchanges, calculating gains/losses, and generating reports for your accountant or government agency.

Understanding how crypto is classified for tax purposes isn't just about paying taxes—it's about planning strategically. Holding long-term can reduce taxes. Transacting frequently without tracking can create audit risk. And misunderstanding the rules can lead to penalties, back taxes, or worse. As crypto continues to evolve, so will tax policy—and those who understand the system will have the edge.

Jasmine's crypto tax story

Jasmine sat hunched over her laptop in a tiny co-working space in Lisbon. It was April 12th, just three days before the U.S. tax deadline, and the browser tabs stacked across her screen told a story of confusion: IRS forms, Reddit threads, crypto tax software comparisons, and a blinking cursor inside an Excel sheet with 426 rows of trades. She rubbed her temples and sipped cold espresso. Last year, crypto was fun—she'd made a killing in altcoins, discovered staking, and even launched her own NFT project. This year, it was overwhelming. Taxes were a beast she hadn't planned for.

Back in 2021, Jasmine had started her crypto journey like many others: she bought Bitcoin on a popular exchange and forgot about it. But by mid-2022, the rabbit hole had deepened. She was trading daily, swapping tokens on decentralized exchanges, earning yield from liquidity pools, and collecting NFTs from up-and-coming artists. It wasn't until her accountant asked for a "cost basis report" that she realized just how complicated things had become.

"What do you mean every trade is taxable?" she had asked, startled.

"Every sale, swap, or even earning of tokens can trigger a tax event," her accountant replied. "Even if you didn't cash out to fiat."

Jasmine was stunned. She had assumed taxes only applied when she withdrew to her bank account. But according to U.S. tax law, crypto was classified as *property*—not currency. That meant every single trade needed to be accounted for: the price at purchase, the price at sale or swap, and the capital gain or loss. She thought about all the times she'd swapped ETH for a new token, or received airdrops from DAOs she didn't even remember joining. It was all taxable.

Things got worse when she realized her staking rewards were also considered income. Even though she hadn't sold those tokens, she owed taxes on their value at the time they were deposited into her wallet. Mining, yield farming, NFT royalties—it was all income in the eyes of the IRS.

Desperate for clarity, Jasmine joined a Telegram group called "Crypto Tax Survivors." There, she met people from around the world sharing their experiences and strategies. A Canadian expat warned her about double taxation. A German user explained the one-year holding rule that exempted long-term holders from capital gains. A couple living in Portugal laughed quietly and said, "We're lucky. No crypto capital gains tax here—for now."

That got Jasmine thinking. Maybe it was time to reconsider where she paid taxes altogether.

She began researching "crypto tax havens"—countries where crypto was treated more favorably. Portugal, the United Arab Emirates, Singapore, and even El Salvador showed up repeatedly. These jurisdictions either didn't tax crypto profits or had lenient rules for long-term holders. Jasmine had already been working remotely—maybe a move made sense. But she also learned that establishing *tax residency* wasn't just about hopping on a plane. It involved meeting physical presence requirements, cutting ties with her home country, and sometimes setting up a local business entity.

The deeper she dove, the more she realized that understanding how crypto was classified wasn't just about filling in the right tax form. It was about reshaping her entire financial life—legally and strategically. She needed better tools, better records, and most of all, a plan.

She subscribed to a crypto tax service and connected all her wallets and exchanges. The imported data made it painfully clear: hundreds of taxable events. Some losses. Some big gains. It also highlighted missed income—staking rewards she hadn't declared, and airdrops she had long forgotten.

Still, Jasmine felt a sense of control returning. The chaos was now structured. The numbers had meaning. She scheduled a meeting with a crypto-savvy accountant who explained how to structure her holdings in the future: holding long-term, reducing unnecessary swaps, and even considering a legal entity for her NFT business. She learned that with proper classification and planning, she could lower her tax bill and stay compliant.

By April 15th, Jasmine clicked "submit" on her tax filing. She didn't love what she owed, but at least she understood *why* she owed it. More importantly, she had a strategy for the year ahead. She was no longer just a crypto enthusiast—she was a tax-aware investor, empowered by clarity and armed with knowledge.

Chapter 2: Taxable Events in Crypto: What Triggers a Tax Bill

One of the most misunderstood aspects of cryptocurrency taxation is knowing when taxes are actually triggered. Crypto users often assume they only owe taxes when they convert their holdings into fiat currency. Unfortunately, this assumption can lead to major tax surprises or compliance issues. In reality, many everyday crypto activities can qualify as **taxable events**—points at which you are required to report a gain, loss, or income.

A taxable event is any action that changes your financial position in a way that requires tax reporting. In traditional finance, this might include selling stocks or receiving a paycheck. In crypto, the rules are broader—and often more complex. The key lies in understanding the difference between a *realized* gain and an *unrealized* gain. You're generally only taxed when you realize a gain, which happens when you dispose of or convert an asset. But the definition of "disposal" is much wider than you might think.

Let's start with the most common taxable events:

1. **Selling crypto for fiat currency** – This is the most obvious case. If you bought Bitcoin at $10,000 and sold

it at $20,000, you have a $10,000 capital gain, which must be reported. If you sell at a loss, that loss can offset gains.

2. **Trading one crypto for another** – Swapping ETH for SOL, or BTC for USDC, is also a taxable event, even if no fiat currency is involved. You've disposed of one asset and acquired another, which means the IRS (and most tax authorities) see this as a realization event.

3. **Using crypto to purchase goods or services** – Buying a laptop with Bitcoin? That's a taxable event. The IRS sees it as if you sold the BTC for cash, then used that cash to buy the item. You must report the fair market value of the BTC at the time of the transaction.

4. **Receiving crypto as income** – If you're paid in crypto for freelance work, consulting, or business sales, you must report the value of the crypto at the time of receipt as income. This income is taxable at your ordinary income rate, and not considered capital gains.

5. **Mining or staking rewards** – Mining rewards are taxed as income when received, based on their fair market value. Staking rewards follow similar rules. Even if you don't sell them, the value must be reported

as income the moment they're deposited into your wallet.

6. **Airdrops and hard forks** – If you receive new coins from an airdrop or hard fork, they may be considered taxable income. The timing of the tax depends on when you gain control over the asset. This rule has caused confusion, especially for passive airdrops.

7. **Crypto lending and yield farming** – Many DeFi protocols pay users yield in the form of tokens. These earnings are taxable as income upon receipt, even if they're not withdrawn. Some tax agencies are still determining how to classify these activities, but in most jurisdictions, receiving tokens of value means income.

8. **Gifts and donations** – Giving or receiving crypto as a gift can have tax implications depending on the amount and the local laws. Large gifts may require a gift tax return. Donating crypto to a registered nonprofit may allow for a deduction, but the transaction still requires documentation.

On the other hand, certain actions are *not* taxable events. These include:

- **Buying crypto with fiat** (e.g., buying ETH with USD)

- **Holding crypto** without selling or swapping
- **Transferring crypto between your own wallets**

However, tracking is still crucial—even for non-taxable events—so that you can properly calculate your cost basis and holding period when a taxable event eventually occurs.

Another hidden trap is **transaction volume**. Even small trades can add up fast, and each one requires tracking of the price at the time of acquisition and the price at the time of sale or swap. Without accurate records, you're essentially guessing on your tax forms, which can lead to errors or audits.

Taxable events vary slightly between jurisdictions. In the U.S., the IRS has issued clear guidelines, but other countries are still adapting. The United Kingdom treats crypto similarly to property. Australia taxes it under capital gains rules, but with exemptions for personal use under $10,000. Singapore, by contrast, does not tax capital gains at all—yet. As more countries develop regulations, understanding what triggers a tax bill becomes essential for global crypto users.

In the fast-evolving crypto world, a single click can trigger a tax obligation. Being aware of which activities are taxable—and which aren't—is the first step to staying compliant and making smart financial decisions. In the next chapter, we'll cover how to calculate your capital gains and losses properly, so that you can file accurately and avoid surprises.

Omar's taxable events.

Omar had always prided himself on being financially literate. He had a background in accounting, ran a small import-export business in Toronto, and had dabbled in the stock market since his early twenties. So when he jumped into crypto in 2020, he figured the same principles would apply. Buy low, sell high, keep records, pay taxes. Simple enough—until it wasn't.

It all started when he downloaded a DeFi wallet and began experimenting with swaps. He converted some ETH into Chainlink, then swapped that for Aave, and so on. What felt like harmless experimentation was actually stacking up tax obligations with every click. In the traditional world, Omar had only been taxed when he sold stock or took profits. But crypto was a different beast. Each trade—no matter how small—was a taxable event.

Things became even more complicated when Omar joined a yield farming protocol. He deposited his tokens into a liquidity pool and started receiving governance tokens as a reward. "Free money," he thought. But his smile faded when his accountant told him those rewards were considered taxable income the moment they were received, even if he didn't cash them out. Worse, the platform had no clear transaction history, and he hadn't written anything down.

"I only got like $300 worth of tokens," he explained. "Why would I owe taxes on that?"

His accountant sighed. "Because the government sees it as income. If someone hands you $300 worth of crypto, they don't care whether you spend it or not—it still counts."

Omar realized he'd unknowingly triggered dozens of taxable events: swaps, staking rewards, even NFT airdrops. He remembered claiming some obscure coin as part of a marketing campaign, never knowing that doing so was a taxable event. To the Canada Revenue Agency (CRA), it didn't matter that he never used the tokens—they had value when received, and that meant taxes were due.

Worse yet, Omar had used crypto to buy a graphics card for his gaming rig. It seemed like a good use of his profits at the time. But again, that transaction triggered a tax event. Because he had used crypto to purchase a good, it was treated as if he'd sold the crypto at market value and then used fiat to buy the item. He had to go back, find the price of the token on the day he spent it, calculate his original cost basis, and determine his gain or loss—all for a single purchase.

The tipping point came when he sold some tokens for USDC. He thought stablecoins weren't taxable because they weren't "real" gains. But that sale counted too. Swapping volatile tokens for stablecoins was still a disposal event, and taxes applied just like any other trade.

Frustrated but determined, Omar took a weekend to clean up his records. He signed up for a crypto tax tool and connected every wallet and exchange he had touched. The platform flagged over 150 taxable events—some as small as $5, others involving hundreds. It took hours, but by the end of the process, he had a complete picture of his crypto activity. He was shocked by how many taxable moments he had simply ignored.

In his accountant's office the next week, he handed over the printed report. "Now that I understand this, I feel like I've been walking through a minefield blindfolded," he admitted.

His accountant chuckled. "Most people are. The rules aren't intuitive, and they change fast. The good news is you caught it early. Many people don't realize they've triggered dozens of taxable events until they're audited."

Omar left that meeting with a newfound respect for tax law. Crypto wasn't just about moonshots and freedom from banks—it also came with responsibility. Going forward, he decided to simplify his strategy. Fewer trades. Longer holds. Proper recordkeeping. And, perhaps most importantly, he would never again assume that a transaction was tax-free just because it wasn't in fiat.

He now understood that in the world of crypto, every token swap, every airdrop, every staking reward could quietly generate a tax bill. And while the freedom of decentralized finance was real, so too were the consequences of not understanding the tax implications that came with it.

Chapter 3: How to Calculate Capital Gains & Losses on Crypto

Calculating capital gains and losses on cryptocurrency can be one of the most daunting parts of tax season, especially for those who have made multiple trades across different platforms. The process involves more than just looking at how much money you made. It requires tracking each transaction, establishing cost basis, determining holding periods, and applying the appropriate tax rules depending on your jurisdiction. But once you understand the core components, calculating gains and losses becomes a repeatable system.

Let's begin with the most important concept: **cost basis**. This is the original value of the asset at the time of acquisition, including any associated fees. If you buy 1 Bitcoin at $10,000 and pay a $100 fee, your cost basis is $10,100. When you sell or exchange that Bitcoin, your capital gain or loss is the difference between your selling price and your cost basis. If you later sell it for $15,000, your gain is $4,900.

The next key element is the **holding period**, which determines whether the gain is classified as short-term or long-term. In the U.S. and many other jurisdictions, assets held for over one year before being sold are considered long-term and are typically taxed at a lower rate. Assets sold within one year are short-term and taxed at your ordinary income tax rate. This creates a strong incentive to hold, especially for those in higher tax brackets.

There are two main types of capital gains:

1. **Realized Gains** – These occur when you sell, swap, or spend your crypto. They are taxable in the year the transaction occurs.

2. **Unrealized Gains** – These are gains on assets you still hold. They are not taxed until you dispose of the asset.

When tracking your trades, it's important to maintain an accurate transaction history. Every trade—no matter how small—needs to be tracked. This includes trades between cryptocurrencies, not just those involving fiat currency. Each of these transactions must be matched to the original acquisition so that cost basis can be calculated.

Here's a simplified example:

- You buy 1 ETH for $2,000
- Later, you trade 0.5 ETH for 100 LINK when ETH is worth $3,000

- Your cost basis for 0.5 ETH was $1,000
- The fair market value at the time of the trade was $1,500
- Your capital gain is $500

Now multiply that process across dozens—or hundreds—of transactions, and you'll see why many investors use crypto tax software like Koinly, CoinTracking, or TokenTax. These tools can import your transactions from exchanges and wallets, calculate gains and losses, and even generate tax forms.

One of the complexities in calculating gains is determining **which coins were sold** when you dispose of part of a position. There are three common accounting methods:

- **FIFO (First-In, First-Out)**: The earliest coins you bought are considered sold first.
- **LIFO (Last-In, First-Out)**: The most recently purchased coins are considered sold first.
- **Specific Identification**: You manually choose which specific coins are sold, typically those with the highest cost basis to reduce your taxable gains.

The method you choose can significantly impact your tax bill. In the U.S., FIFO is the default unless you specify otherwise. In other countries, the method may vary or may not be clearly defined, so consult a tax professional if unsure.

You can also use **capital losses** to offset gains. If you sold a coin at a loss, you can subtract that amount from your gains to reduce your total taxable income. In many countries, you can carry unused losses forward to future years. However, you cannot claim a loss if you immediately buy the same asset back—this is known as a "wash sale" rule in traditional finance, though it's not yet consistently enforced in crypto. Still, laws are evolving, and it's wise to avoid aggressive loss-harvesting without professional guidance.

Lastly, remember that **fees matter**. Transaction fees on exchanges, gas fees for blockchain interactions, and platform charges can often be added to your cost basis or subtracted from your proceeds. Don't overlook them—they can significantly reduce your taxable gain.

The bottom line is this: accurately calculating capital gains and losses isn't just about compliance. It's about understanding your financial picture, planning your trades strategically, and avoiding costly mistakes. With clean records and the right tools, crypto taxes become manageable—and even offer opportunities for optimization.

Sophie, the crypto enthusiast

Sophie had always been meticulous with numbers. As a former bookkeeper turned crypto enthusiast, she thought she had a solid grasp on how to manage her portfolio. But in the spring of 2024, while preparing her taxes in her small San Diego apartment, she realized just how far behind she had fallen. Not in trading—she was ahead of the game there—but in understanding how those trades translated into taxable gains and losses. And now, the IRS wanted to know.

Her crypto journey began modestly—some BTC on Coinbase, a few ETH purchases on Kraken. But by late 2022, she had expanded into DEXs, tried her hand at yield farming, and even flipped some NFTs. Every transaction had seemed like a step toward financial independence. But as she stared at her spreadsheet, she saw a nightmare of numbers—random buys, countless swaps, and no consistent records.

Her friend Luis had told her about tax software, but Sophie wasn't ready to hand over the reins yet. She wanted to *understand* how the math worked. So she poured over IRS guidance and tax forums, discovering the critical concept of cost basis. Every time she bought a coin, that purchase price—plus any fees—became her baseline. Sell above that, and she had a gain. Sell below, and it was a loss.

It made sense in theory. In practice? It was chaos. She had bought MATIC on three different days at three different prices and sold half of it later during a mini bull run. But which MATIC had she sold? The ones she bought at $0.80? The ones at $1.20? Depending on her method—FIFO, LIFO, or specific identification—her taxable gain would swing by hundreds of dollars.

She sat back, sipping green tea, and ran the numbers both ways. FIFO showed a $700 gain. LIFO showed only $250. She now understood why accounting method mattered so much. Most countries defaulted to FIFO unless you declared otherwise. But she didn't remember ever making a choice. Was she stuck?

She called a tax advisor who specialized in crypto. He explained that with the right documentation, she could elect specific identification and strategically sell coins with the highest cost basis—what some called the HIFO (highest-in, first-out) method. That minimized gains. But it required thorough recordkeeping—down to the time and date of each purchase.

Sophie's brain throbbed as she thought of all the gas fees she had forgotten to include. Those, the advisor said, could be added to her cost basis or deducted as expenses if properly documented. So she spent hours going through her MetaMask and Phantom wallets, copying fee data from block explorers. She even found a $400 gas fee from a failed DeFi swap she had totally blocked out. Could she write that off? Maybe, maybe not.

She ran a simulation using a crypto tax app. After inputting everything manually—every swap, every fee, every date—she had a full picture of her gains and losses. Some were big. Some were surprising. She had forgotten about the small tokens she had dumped during the bear market. Those losses, it turned out, could offset her gains. And because she hadn't used them in previous years, she could carry them forward.

For the first time in weeks, Sophie smiled. This wasn't just about taxes—it was about understanding her entire financial life. She printed the report and highlighted her long-term gains in green and short-term ones in red. Holding for over a year had saved her nearly 15% in taxes. If she'd sold everything in a panic last fall, the bill would have been devastating.

The final piece clicked when she realized she could plan for next year. She could track everything in real time, label each coin with its purchase details, and even organize her trades by accounting method. It wasn't easy, but it was empowering.

By the time she filed her return, Sophie wasn't just compliant—she was confident. She now saw capital gains and losses not as a confusing tax burden, but as a strategic tool. And as she looked at her portfolio, she saw more than just coins. She saw opportunity, clarity, and control.

Chapter 4: Crypto Income: Mining, Staking, and Airdrops Explained

As the crypto economy evolves beyond simple buying and selling, more users are engaging in activities that generate crypto-based income—without traditional employment or centralized intermediaries. These income streams include **mining**, **staking**, and **airdrops**, and while they may seem like free money, tax authorities do not view them that way. In fact, most of these activities are taxed as *income* when received, and in many jurisdictions, they must be reported at the fair market value on the day you gain control of the asset.

Let's begin with **mining**, one of the oldest and most well-known forms of crypto income. Whether you're running a single GPU rig at home or operating an industrial mining farm, the income generated from successfully validating blocks is considered taxable. The fair market value of the mined coins at the time you receive them must be reported as ordinary income. For example, if you mine 0.1 BTC and it's worth $2,500 at the time it enters your wallet, that $2,500 is taxable income—even if you don't sell the Bitcoin. Later, if you sell the coin, you'll also owe capital gains taxes on any increase in value from the day you received it. That means mining crypto can result in *two* taxable events: once when received (income), and again when sold (capital gain or loss).

Staking is the proof-of-stake counterpart to mining, and it works similarly from a tax perspective. When you stake coins like ETH, ADA, or SOL and receive rewards, the value of those rewards at the moment they're credited to your wallet must be reported as income. This applies whether you're staking solo, through a validator, or using centralized platforms like Coinbase or Binance. And just like mining, if the coins appreciate in value and you later sell them, you'll owe capital gains taxes on the difference. Many users make the mistake of only tracking the sale—but the IRS and other tax agencies are increasingly focused on when rewards are *received*, not just sold.

Airdrops are another common source of crypto income, but they often catch people off guard. Airdrops occur when new tokens are distributed to users for free—usually as a reward for holding a specific asset, participating in a protocol, or even just being part of a community. While airdrops may feel like gifts, they are often treated as income the moment you have access to the tokens. For example, if you receive 1,000 tokens worth $0.50 each, you must report $500 of income, even if you never sell them. The problem? Many users don't realize they've received an airdrop—or the value drops quickly, leaving them with a tax bill but little actual profit.

This also applies to **hard forks**, which occur when a blockchain splits and creates a new asset (like Bitcoin Cash from Bitcoin). If you gain control over a new asset due to a hard fork, the IRS considers that taxable income at the time of access. Even if you didn't ask for the forked token, if it lands in your wallet and you can spend it, it becomes taxable.

One of the biggest challenges in dealing with crypto income is **recordkeeping**. Unlike traditional income—where you receive a W-2 or 1099—crypto income often goes unreported unless you manually track it. That means it's your responsibility to note the fair market value, time of receipt, and source of income. Failing to do so can lead to incorrect filings or missed income reports, which might trigger audits or penalties.

The type of crypto income also affects **self-employment tax**. In the U.S., for instance, mining rewards are not just subject to income tax—they may also trigger self-employment taxes if the mining is done as a business. That adds another layer of complexity and potential tax liability, especially for large-scale operations or consistent earners.

To reduce tax exposure, some users choose to run their crypto income operations under a legal entity, such as an LLC or corporation. This can open up deductions for electricity, equipment, and other business expenses, but it also comes with additional legal and tax reporting requirements. As always, speak with a tax professional if you're unsure.

Finally, don't ignore **airdrop scams and spam tokens**, which sometimes appear in wallets unannounced. If you didn't claim or control the asset, you may not have to report it. However, if you sell even one of those tokens or interact with the contract, that may be considered acceptance and can trigger tax obligations. Exercise caution and don't blindly engage with unknown tokens.

In summary, mining, staking, and airdrops are powerful tools for building wealth in crypto—but they also come with significant tax responsibilities. Knowing how and when to report these income streams can help you avoid penalties and position yourself to take advantage of future opportunities in a compliant, sustainable way.

Now, let's go over Liam's story

Liam's garage always smelled faintly of ozone and hot metal. Rows of whirring GPU miners lined his workbench like loyal little soldiers, glowing with multicolored LED lights. For the last two years, he had been mining Ethereum—first as a hobby, then as a side hustle, and eventually as a full-fledged business. He loved the autonomy. No boss, no clock, just him and the network. But as the machines hummed away, his inbox buzzed with something far less satisfying: a tax notice from the IRS.

He had expected a small adjustment, maybe a few hundred dollars. But the letter said he owed thousands. Why? Because he had never reported his mined ETH as *income*—just the profits when he sold. He had misunderstood how crypto earnings worked. Now he was learning the hard way that mining rewards are taxed the moment they're received, based on their fair market value. It didn't matter whether he sold them or held onto them for a year. The IRS wanted their share the moment his wallet filled up.

Liam reached out to a tax consultant who specialized in crypto. She asked him for detailed records—date, time, value of each mining payout. He didn't have them. His mining software tracked hashes, not tax data. The exchange he used only logged deposits. "You need more than just wallet activity," she explained. "You need *income recognition*—how much your mined coins were worth when you received them." That meant pulling historical price data and mapping it to his reward timestamps. It felt like a second job.

Things got even more complicated when Liam realized that some of his income might be subject to *self-employment tax* as well. Because he was mining as a business—buying equipment, paying for electricity, reinvesting profits—he was considered a sole proprietor in the eyes of the IRS. That meant his crypto income wasn't just ordinary income. It was *business income*, with added obligations.

Meanwhile, his girlfriend, Priya, was learning her own hard lesson with **staking**. She had been earning passive income by staking her ADA on a mobile wallet. The rewards were modest—$80 here, $120 there—but consistent. She had assumed that, like a savings account, those rewards weren't taxable until withdrawn. Wrong. Her accountant explained that staking rewards are taxed the moment they're deposited, not when sold. She had dozens of small taxable events, none of which she had tracked. Fortunately, her wallet had a built-in export feature, which saved her hours of frustration.

Their friend Malik faced yet another variation of the same problem—**airdrops**. He had received 2,000 tokens from a DAO he supported but never paid them much attention. He didn't even know their value had spiked to $1.75 each at one point. When he finally checked his wallet, they were worth $0.12 each. He shrugged and sold them for a quick buck. What he didn't realize was that the IRS wanted taxes based on the *value when received*, not when sold. That meant reporting $3,500 in income—even though he only made about $250 from the sale. It felt unfair, but the law was clear: airdrops are income the moment you can access and use the tokens.

One night, the three friends gathered in Liam's garage, laptops open, comparing horror stories and organizing records. They had all learned the same lesson in different ways: *crypto income is real income*, and it doesn't matter whether it comes from mining rigs, validator rewards, or unexpected airdrops. They began using tracking software, marking each taxable event, and even planning for a business entity to help with deductions.

Liam discovered he could deduct his electric bills and hardware purchases if he filed properly. Priya learned to report staking income quarterly to avoid underpayment penalties. Malik set up a system to monitor his wallets and flag unexpected token arrivals before they became tax landmines.

It wasn't just about staying out of trouble anymore. It was about becoming professionals in a growing, decentralized economy. As the tax rules evolved, so would they—more prepared, more aware, and more in control of their digital income.

Chapter 5: Crypto Tax Reporting Requirements: Forms, Records & Deadlines

Filing taxes with crypto holdings and transactions is no longer an optional gray area—it's a legal obligation in most jurisdictions. While early adopters may have enjoyed years of limited oversight, the global crackdown on crypto tax evasion is well underway. Today, governments are tightening regulations, issuing warnings, and even sharing exchange data to track taxpayers. As such, understanding **which forms to file**, **what records to keep**, and **when deadlines apply** is essential for staying compliant and stress-free during tax season.

Let's begin with the **United States**, where the Internal Revenue Service (IRS) has made its position on cryptocurrency clear: it is considered property and subject to both income and capital gains taxes. Every U.S. tax return now includes a direct question—"At any time during the year, did you receive, sell, send, exchange, or otherwise acquire any financial interest in any virtual currency?" This question appears on the front page of IRS Form 1040. Answering falsely can lead to legal consequences, even if no crypto tax is owed.

If you've made crypto trades, you'll generally need to complete **Form 8949**, which reports capital gains and losses from the sale or exchange of property. Each row represents a single transaction and must include:

- Description of the asset (e.g., 0.5 BTC)
- Date acquired
- Date sold
- Proceeds (sale amount)
- Cost basis (purchase amount)
- Gain or loss

The totals from Form 8949 flow into **Schedule D**, which summarizes your overall capital gains and losses. If you had multiple transactions—especially from exchanges—crypto tax software can generate a completed Form 8949, making this step much easier.

If you received crypto as income—such as from mining, staking, freelance work, or airdrops—you may also need to report it on **Schedule 1** (Additional Income) or **Schedule C** if you're running a business. For business income, the IRS may require **self-employment tax**, which includes Social Security and Medicare contributions.

Those who receive crypto payments above $10,000 in a single transaction may also fall under **Form 8300** reporting requirements for large cash transactions. And if your crypto is held on a foreign exchange or wallet, **FBAR (FinCEN Form 114)** or **FATCA (Form 8938)** may apply if balances exceed certain thresholds. These international compliance requirements can catch investors off guard and carry severe penalties if ignored.

Other countries have similar or emerging requirements. For example:

- **United Kingdom (HMRC)**: Requires capital gains reporting on self-assessment tax returns. There's no dedicated crypto form, but detailed records are essential.

- **Canada (CRA)**: Treats crypto as a commodity; uses capital gains forms and requires all income to be reported, including mining and airdrops.

- **Australia (ATO)**: Requires capital gains tax on most crypto disposals, with tracking of cost basis and holding periods.

- **Germany**: Crypto is tax-free if held for over a year, but trades within that period must be reported.

Regardless of your location, the single most important habit is **maintaining accurate records**. These should include:

- Date and time of each transaction
- Amount and type of crypto involved
- USD (or local currency) value at the time
- Cost basis and proceeds
- Purpose of the transaction (purchase, sale, reward, airdrop, etc.)
- Associated fees (gas, transaction, and platform fees)

Using **crypto tax software** like Koinly, CoinLedger, or TokenTax can automate much of this process by connecting to wallets and exchanges, categorizing activity, and producing tax-ready documents. Many tools also allow you to preview potential tax outcomes before selling assets, helping with strategic planning.

Deadlines matter. In the U.S., the individual tax deadline is typically **April 15**, though it may shift slightly depending on holidays or weekends. Filing extensions are available but do not extend the payment due date. Late filings or underpayment of taxes—even due to crypto mistakes—can result in penalties and interest. Other countries have their own timelines, but many align with the April–June window for annual tax filings.

It's also smart to **reconcile quarterly**, especially if you're actively trading or earning rewards. This allows for better tax planning, estimated payments, and avoiding the end-of-year scramble. Crypto is volatile—delaying tracking often leads to inaccuracies and missed deductions.

In summary, as crypto tax enforcement ramps up, being proactive is key. Know the forms you need, track your records in real time, and seek help from professionals or software tools when necessary. With the right habits and preparation, tax reporting can become a manageable—and even strategic—part of your crypto journey.

Tasha and Form 8949

Tasha sat at her kitchen table, tax documents spread out like a financial battlefield. Her morning coffee had gone cold as she stared at the IRS website, trying to decode the alphabet soup of forms: 8949, Schedule D, Schedule 1, 1040. She'd always filed her taxes on her own—simple W-2, a few deductions, done in under an hour. But this year was different. This year, she had crypto.

It started innocently enough—just a few Ethereum purchases on Coinbase, a couple NFT flips, and some staking rewards. Then she'd tried DeFi lending. Then she joined a DAO. Now, she had activity across six platforms, dozens of trades, and no idea how to organize any of it for tax season.

Her first realization came when she logged into TurboTax and saw a new question on the front page: *"Did you receive, sell, send, exchange, or otherwise acquire any financial interest in cryptocurrency?"* There was no way around it. She had to say "yes."

Tasha assumed it would ask her for one summary number—total profit or loss—but the program asked for every single trade: date acquired, date sold, cost basis, proceeds, gain or loss. "Are they serious?" she muttered aloud, flipping through her jumbled spreadsheet.

She called her older cousin Derrick, who worked in finance. "It's not optional," he said flatly. "They added that question to flag crypto holders. If you answer no, and they find out otherwise, it could be considered tax fraud."

That hit her hard. She wasn't trying to cheat—she just didn't know what to do. Derrick explained that she needed **Form 8949** to report every crypto disposal. Each time she sold, swapped, or spent crypto, it triggered a capital gain or loss. "The totals go into Schedule D," he added, "but 8949 is where all the details go."

She opened her wallets and exchanges, trying to find a way to download her history. Some had CSV exports. Others didn't. She had made so many small trades, some under $50, that she thought didn't matter. But every one was required. Every trade, every gas fee, every reward. She had even used ETH to buy an NFT—which counted as a sale for tax purposes.

Then there were her **staking rewards**. She'd received about $700 worth of crypto last year. "That's income," Derrick said. "Report it on Schedule 1. If you were staking regularly, the IRS might expect self-employment tax too."

The worst part? She had received a few **airdrops**—tokens she didn't ask for, sitting forgotten in her wallet. She hadn't sold them, but apparently, the IRS still expected her to report their value at the time she had access. That meant finding the price of obscure tokens on random days from six months ago. She sighed and looked at the clock. Midnight.

A friend recommended she try a crypto tax software app. Skeptical but desperate, she connected her wallets and exchanges. After 30 minutes of syncing, the dashboard displayed her full crypto history: 98 taxable events, $1,400 in income, $3,700 in capital gains, and $890 in losses. She was shocked by how much was there. It even generated a complete Form 8949 and calculated her total gains and losses. The headache began to lift.

Tasha filed an extension to buy more time and promised herself she'd do it differently next year. From now on, she would track her activity in real time, save all CSV files, and reconcile her transactions quarterly. She even considered starting a small LLC to formalize her staking and DeFi income. Derrick explained that doing so could open up deductions—hardware, internet, gas fees, even a portion of her rent if she filed correctly.

The experience transformed her. What started as confusion became empowerment. She wasn't afraid of taxes anymore—she understood them. And that understanding gave her confidence to keep growing her crypto portfolio, but now with structure, foresight, and total control.

Chapter 6: Crypto Taxes Around the World: Jurisdictional Differences & Tax Havens

Cryptocurrency is global by nature, but tax laws are *not*. One of the biggest mistakes crypto users make is assuming the tax rules in their home country apply everywhere. In reality, every country treats crypto differently—some favorably, others harshly. Whether you're a digital nomad, remote worker, business owner, or investor, understanding the **jurisdictional differences** in crypto taxation can be the difference between keeping your profits and losing them to the taxman.

Let's begin with the **United States**, where cryptocurrency is treated as property and subject to capital gains and income tax. The IRS requires detailed reporting for every taxable event, including trades, income, staking rewards, airdrops, and NFT sales. Long-term capital gains are taxed at lower rates (0–20%), while short-term gains and income are taxed at your ordinary rate. The U.S. also has strict foreign asset reporting laws under FATCA and FBAR, and U.S. citizens are taxed on their *worldwide income*, even if they live abroad.

In contrast, the **United Kingdom** treats crypto as property under HMRC guidance. Capital gains tax applies when selling, swapping, or gifting crypto, while income tax applies to mining, staking, and airdrops. HMRC allows pooling of assets for cost basis but requires detailed records for every transaction. There is an annual capital gains tax allowance, but gains beyond that threshold are taxed progressively.

Canada treats crypto as a commodity. Trades are taxed under capital gains rules, but frequent trading or mining could be classified as business income—taxed at higher rates with no preferential treatment. Canada also does not allow like-kind exchanges, and strict reporting is expected. Failure to declare income can lead to harsh penalties and interest.

Germany offers a unique opportunity: if you hold crypto for over one year, any gains are tax-free for individuals. However, if you sell within a year and the profit exceeds €600, taxes apply. Mining, staking, and business activity are taxed as income. This makes Germany an attractive location for long-term HODLers but risky for active traders.

Portugal is often hailed as a crypto tax haven. As of this writing, private individuals face no capital gains tax on crypto sales, and most staking rewards and airdrops are also tax-exempt. However, Portugal is evolving its laws, and professional trading or business activity may eventually be subject to taxation. Digital nomads flock here for the low tax burden, but changes are on the horizon.

Switzerland, known for its favorable financial climate, classifies crypto as personal wealth. There is no capital gains tax for private individuals, but wealth tax applies based on total holdings. Staking and mining may be subject to income tax. Swiss cantons also have local autonomy, creating regional variations in crypto policy.

Singapore offers another crypto-friendly jurisdiction. There is no capital gains tax, and long-term holding is completely tax-free. Businesses that deal in crypto as part of operations are taxed on profits, but individuals enjoy significant freedom. This has made Singapore a hub for crypto startups and investors.

Meanwhile, **United Arab Emirates (UAE)**—especially Dubai and Abu Dhabi—offers tax-free status for many types of crypto activity. No income tax, no capital gains tax, and no reporting on crypto trades for residents in designated free zones. Residency and business visas are available to crypto investors and entrepreneurs, making the UAE an attractive jurisdiction for wealth preservation.

On the other end of the spectrum are countries like **India**, which has introduced a 30% flat tax on all crypto gains—without allowing loss offsets. Every transaction is taxed, and there's an additional 1% tax deducted at source (TDS) on certain transfers. This has led many Indian crypto users to move assets abroad or relocate entirely.

China, while hostile toward crypto trading, is still in the process of defining its taxation framework. The government has banned most forms of crypto use, but taxes may apply in cases where activity is detected. Similarly, **Russia** has proposed aggressive regulation and taxation, with mandatory reporting for holdings over certain thresholds.

If you're a crypto user considering **relocation**, pay close attention to *tax residency rules*. Simply spending time in a tax haven doesn't mean you're exempt. Most countries define tax residency by physical presence (e.g., 183-day rule), center of vital interests, or legal domicile. Some countries tax citizens on worldwide income regardless of residence (e.g., the U.S.), while others only tax residents.

Setting up **offshore entities** or **international bank accounts** doesn't automatically reduce tax obligations. In fact, doing so incorrectly can trigger reporting requirements and scrutiny. Legal tax optimization requires planning, transparency, and compliance—not secrecy.

In conclusion, crypto tax treatment is one of the most important strategic factors in managing your wealth. By understanding the differences between countries—and planning accordingly—you can legally reduce your tax burden, preserve more of your gains, and align your lifestyle with your financial goals. The right jurisdiction can turn a good crypto year into a great one, while the wrong one can wipe out your profits in taxes.

Diego's story

Diego stood on the balcony of his rented flat in Lisbon, sipping espresso and watching the orange rooftops shimmer in the morning sun. He had just finished a video call with his accountant back in California, and for the first time in years, he felt financially free. Not because his portfolio had exploded—though it had doubled last year—but because he had finally stopped hemorrhaging money on taxes. Moving to Portugal had changed everything.

Only twelve months earlier, Diego was drowning in crypto tax obligations. He had built a successful business around NFT consulting and trading digital assets, and while his earnings were solid, his U.S. tax bill was brutal. Income tax, self-employment tax, short-term capital gains—it felt like the IRS was taking a third of everything he made. He had heard whispers online about crypto tax havens, but he never thought they were real options—until he hit his breaking point.

"I just want to keep more of what I earn," he told his tax advisor during a particularly frustrating Zoom call. "Isn't there anywhere on Earth where I'm not punished for being successful?"

His advisor paused, then carefully replied, "Have you ever considered becoming a tax resident somewhere else? Portugal, for example?"

That question sparked a journey. Diego began researching international tax laws, moving beyond Reddit threads and into whitepapers, legal documents, and global residency programs. What he discovered shocked him: some countries not only tolerated crypto—they welcomed it.

Portugal, where he now stood, was a prime example. Private individuals paid **no capital gains tax** on crypto holdings. Staking income? Often ignored. Trading activity? Lightly regulated at most. As long as you weren't operating a formal crypto business, the Portuguese government largely stayed out of your way. No endless forms. No 8949. No FATCA. It was freedom—and it was legal.

He joined Telegram groups for expats, consulted immigration lawyers, and eventually applied for the D7 visa, which granted residency based on passive or freelance income. Within months, he had secured a place to live, updated his legal address, and opened a local bank account. He had never felt more in control of his finances.

But Diego wasn't naïve. He learned that **residency rules** varied everywhere. In some countries, 183 days was enough. In others, it was about the "center of vital interests"—where you worked, banked, and had personal ties. He cut unnecessary ties to the U.S., kept his trips back short, and documented everything. He didn't want any ambiguity if ever audited.

From Portugal, he met other crypto expats who had found homes in **Dubai**, **Singapore**, and **Switzerland**. An Italian developer he met at a café had moved to the UAE, enjoying tax-free earnings in Dubai's crypto-friendly free zones. A French coder was loving life in Singapore, where capital gains were a foreign concept. Others were eyeing Puerto Rico, where U.S. citizens could reduce federal tax burdens without giving up their passports—if they met strict requirements under Acts 60 and 20.

Yet, not all stories were inspiring. One developer from India had moved to Thailand in hopes of avoiding India's harsh 30%

crypto tax. But because he hadn't changed his tax residency properly, he still owed taxes back home—and penalties for failing to report airdrops. Another trader, based in Germany, thought he was tax-free after a year of holding, only to learn that frequent margin trading reclassified his activity as a business under local law.

Diego took notes. He hired a cross-border tax consultant to help him stay compliant on both sides. He wasn't trying to hide. He was building a global business and wanted to play by the rules—just in a place with smarter ones.

He now spent his days running webinars, consulting for NFT projects, and investing long-term—all from his laptop. No heavy tax burdens. No fear of audits. He felt like he had stepped into the future—where money was borderless, and freedom wasn't just about financial gains, but about having the *right strategy in the right country.*

Crypto had opened the door. International tax knowledge had turned the key. And now, Diego's wealth was not only growing—it was protected.

Chapter 7: Legal Structures for Crypto Businesses and Investors

As cryptocurrency matures from speculative investment to full-fledged industry, many participants find themselves moving beyond casual trading into more formal business activity. Whether you're launching a token, operating a mining operation, offering staking-as-a-service, flipping NFTs, or managing a DAO treasury, you may benefit from establishing a **legal structure** to protect your assets, limit liability, and optimize taxes.

The first and most common structure for solo crypto entrepreneurs is the **Limited Liability Company (LLC)**. In jurisdictions like the U.S., an LLC is relatively easy to form and provides personal liability protection. That means your personal bank accounts and assets are separate from business debts or legal disputes. For crypto miners, validators, consultants, and content creators, forming an LLC can legitimize operations and unlock tax advantages like business deductions for internet, equipment, software, and electricity.

However, LLCs have default tax treatment as “pass-through” entities, meaning income is taxed on your personal return unless you elect otherwise. In some cases, particularly with larger earnings or reinvestments, you might opt for an

S-corporation (in the U.S.), which can reduce self-employment taxes and allow you to pay yourself a salary plus distributions. But this comes with increased compliance, payroll setup, and stricter documentation.

Crypto investors managing large portfolios or working with other partners often consider **Limited Partnerships (LPs)** or **C-corporations**. These structures are useful for venture capital-style investing, pooled funds, or service-based crypto companies. A C-corporation, while subject to double taxation in the U.S., can offer flexibility for international investors, stock issuance, and potential future acquisitions. In the startup world, many crypto founders choose Delaware C-corps for raising venture capital—even if they live abroad.

Internationally, jurisdictions like **Switzerland**, **Singapore**, **Estonia**, and **the British Virgin Islands (BVI)** have become popular hubs for incorporating crypto companies due to their clear digital asset regulations, favorable tax regimes, and business-friendly environments. However, just setting up a company offshore does *not* make your income tax-free. You must also sever tax residency from your home country and comply with local substance requirements, including office leases, employees, or active management.

For **DAOs (Decentralized Autonomous Organizations)**,

legal structuring is still evolving. Some DAOs operate without any legal wrapper, which can expose members to personal liability. Others choose to incorporate as LLCs in **Wyoming**, which became the first U.S. state to recognize DAOs as legal entities. This allows the DAO to sign contracts, own IP, and open bank accounts. However, DAO governance and compliance still require internal rules, off-chain administration, and clarity around fiduciary duties and taxation.

Crypto hedge funds, NFT projects, and Web3 startups may also establish **foundation structures**, particularly in Switzerland (Zug), the Cayman Islands, or Panama. These nonprofit-like entities are used to manage open-source projects, treasury reserves, and token allocations while maintaining decentralization. However, they are complex to set up, costly to maintain, and require legal guidance to avoid abuse or regulatory challenges.

In all cases, it's critical to consider the **tax treatment** of the entity. Where is it tax-resident? What income is reported? Are crypto transactions recognized as business income, capital gains, or something else? And how are the owners paid—salary, dividends, or crypto distributions? These questions must be addressed upfront to avoid messy audits or double taxation down the road.

Additionally, setting up the right legal structure opens the door to traditional tools like **business banking**, **credit**, **insurance**, and **contracts**. This is especially important for investors working with other people's money, raising capital, or operating platforms. Without a legal shield, one mistake could lead to lawsuits or tax liabilities that impact your personal finances.

Finally, **regulatory clarity** is still catching up. New laws in the EU, U.K., U.S., and Asia are evolving fast. Depending on what your crypto business does—issue tokens, manage wallets, process payments, offer financial services—you may need licenses or registrations (e.g., MSB, VASP, EMI, etc.). Skipping this step could put you on the wrong side of enforcement.

In summary, setting up the right legal structure for your crypto activity isn't just about compliance—it's about control, protection, scalability, and peace of mind. Whether you're a solo operator or a growing team, taking this step transforms your crypto hustle into a legitimate, future-ready business.

Amara's startup

Amara never imagined she'd become the CEO of a crypto analytics startup. Just a year ago, she was posting free trading insights on Twitter and running a Telegram group for beginners. But as her content gained traction, sponsors came calling, clients requested consulting, and a friend offered to partner with her to build a dashboard for NFT market trends. That's when it hit her—this wasn't a side hustle anymore. It was a business. And she had no legal structure.

At first, she shrugged it off. Everything was going well—money was flowing in through stablecoins, she had a hot wallet for expenses, and she tracked her income in a spreadsheet. But then, two things happened that forced her to get serious. First, a major brand asked to sign a contract with her... but insisted they could only work with incorporated businesses. Second, she got a notice from her crypto exchange flagging suspicious activity and requesting documentation. Her personal wallet had received over $100,000 in revenue, and compliance systems had taken notice.

She reached out to her friend, a crypto lawyer in New York. "You're making real money," he said. "If something goes wrong—if someone sues you, if a smart contract fails—you're personally liable unless you form a business entity." He explained that a **Limited Liability Company (LLC)** would protect her personal assets and create a legal separation between herself and the business. Plus, it would open doors to banking, credit, and even investment.

Amara registered an LLC in Wyoming, one of the most

crypto-friendly states in the U.S. The process was fast, affordable, and online. Soon after, she opened a business bank account, created a bookkeeping system, and started paying herself a small salary from the LLC. For the first time, her operation felt official—and safe.

She wasn't alone. At a crypto founders' meetup in Austin, she met developers who had formed **C-corporations** to attract venture capital. They wanted to build DeFi apps and needed a scalable structure for equity, token allocation, and legal clarity. Others had formed **DAOs** and were exploring Wyoming's new DAO LLC registration, which gave them a legal wrapper for a decentralized project. "We used to run this from a multisig wallet," one founder said. "Now we have bylaws, a registered agent, and even a legal budget."

Amara also met a German investor who ran a crypto hedge fund through a **BVI (British Virgin Islands) entity**, using nominee directors and offshore banking. While impressed, Amara felt the complexity was too much for her needs. "I'm not trying to hide," she said. "I just want to be compliant and protected."

Still, the idea of global structuring stuck with her. She spoke with an advisor about **Singapore**, where startups could incorporate with minimal tax on crypto gains, and

Switzerland, home to "Crypto Valley" in Zug. These jurisdictions welcomed crypto innovation and offered clearer legal frameworks than most Western countries. If her startup grew, she could open a subsidiary or relocate part of her operations.

Then came the questions about taxes. Her lawyer explained that business income was taxed differently than personal capital gains. She could now deduct legitimate expenses—software subscriptions, computer equipment, gas fees for wallets, travel to crypto conferences. But she had to keep records. Good records. So she hired a bookkeeper and started using an accounting platform integrated with her wallets.

One night, she got an email from a DeFi protocol requesting a formal partnership. They asked her to sign an agreement, submit invoices, and pass KYC checks for B2B transactions. Just a year ago, she would've panicked. Now, she forwarded the email to her lawyer and finance team. Her LLC had a contract template. Her invoices had tax IDs. Her business was ready.

For Amara, forming a legal structure wasn't just about compliance—it was about *maturity*. She had turned her crypto hustle into a real, scalable company. It didn't slow her down—it accelerated her growth. And in an industry full of uncertainty, that clarity felt like an edge.

Chapter 8: Staying Compliant: Audits, Penalties, and Risk Reduction Strategies

As governments around the world catch up to the scale and complexity of cryptocurrency markets, tax agencies have begun enforcing compliance with increasing scrutiny. The days of flying under the radar are rapidly disappearing. Whether you're a casual investor or a full-time crypto entrepreneur, **staying compliant** is no longer optional—it's essential to protecting your assets and peace of mind. This chapter outlines how to avoid audits, minimize penalties, and stay one step ahead with effective risk management strategies.

Let's begin with **audits**. In most countries, tax authorities like the IRS (U.S.), HMRC (U.K.), CRA (Canada), and ATO (Australia) can audit your financial records for several years after you file a return. While not every crypto holder will face an audit, certain red flags increase the likelihood. These include unusually high reported gains, frequent trading with no reported income, discrepancies between exchange-reported data and your own filings, or failing to answer crypto-related questions honestly on your tax return.

One of the simplest ways to reduce audit risk is by maintaining **accurate, organized records**. This includes detailed logs of all crypto transactions: dates, amounts, cost basis, proceeds, fair market value, and associated fees. Whether you use a spreadsheet, crypto tax software, or a professional accountant, your records should be easy to access, audit-ready, and updated regularly. Failing to maintain proper documentation is one of the fastest ways to lose an audit—even if your intent was honest.

If you are **audited**, be prepared to provide not only your reported data but also **supporting evidence**—exchange statements, blockchain explorer screenshots, tax software reports, and records of fiat conversions. In many jurisdictions, the burden of proof is on you, not the government. If you can't show where your crypto came from or how you valued it, the agency may make assumptions in their favor.

Then there are the **penalties**. These can range from mild fines for late filings to substantial interest charges for underreporting income. In serious cases, especially those involving willful evasion or large unreported gains, criminal penalties—including jail time—are possible. While rare, cases have already occurred where investors and traders have faced legal consequences for ignoring their crypto tax obligations. The safest path is **early disclosure** and voluntary correction if you discover a mistake.

Many governments offer **voluntary disclosure programs** (VDPs) or **amnesty periods**. These allow taxpayers to come forward, correct past errors, and pay owed taxes with reduced or waived penalties. If you've never reported your crypto income or suspect you made a mistake, it's wise to act quickly. Waiting until the government contacts you eliminates the option to disclose voluntarily.

Another powerful risk reduction strategy is **estimated tax payments**. In jurisdictions like the U.S., if you expect to owe more than a certain amount in taxes, you're required to make quarterly estimated payments. This applies especially to individuals who earn staking income, receive freelance payments in crypto, or trade frequently. Failing to make estimated payments can lead to underpayment penalties, even if you file your return on time. Planning ahead and setting aside a percentage of crypto income for taxes each quarter can prevent surprises later.

For crypto businesses and self-employed individuals, **segregating funds** is key. Maintain separate wallets for personal use and business operations. Create a "tax wallet" where you transfer a percentage of each income event for safekeeping. These practices not only improve compliance but make it easier to manage cash flow and reduce audit exposure.

Also, keep in mind that **exchange reporting rules** are tightening. Major platforms are now required to send transaction data directly to tax agencies, often without notifying users. In the U.S., new legislation under the Infrastructure Investment and Jobs Act expands reporting obligations for brokers, potentially including DEXs and wallet providers. The result is greater transparency—and less room for noncompliance.

Internationally, the **OECD's Crypto-Asset Reporting Framework (CARF)** is being adopted by many countries. This global agreement will create standardized data sharing between tax authorities, much like FATCA and CRS for banking. Even if you move abroad, your crypto activities may still be reported back to your home country.

Lastly, working with **qualified professionals** can save you far more than it costs. A crypto-savvy accountant can help you structure your activities, ensure proper classification of income vs. capital gains, and keep you informed of evolving rules. Legal advisors can help with business formation, cross-border structuring, and audit defense.

In short, compliance is no longer a niche concern—it's a foundational element of building and preserving crypto wealth. By understanding how audits work, how penalties arise, and how to plan proactively, you can protect everything you've built and thrive in an increasingly regulated environment.

Tariq's penalty relief options

Tariq had never worried much about taxes. A talented blockchain developer and early investor in multiple altcoins, he had always focused more on building and HODLing than reporting. To him, crypto was a revolution, not something meant to be buried in paperwork. But that illusion shattered one Monday morning when a letter from the Internal Revenue Service arrived, bearing the word *Audit* in bold.

His heart sank. He had filed his taxes the previous year through a standard online service, inputting basic numbers from memory and hoping for the best. He hadn't kept detailed transaction records, hadn't used tax software, and certainly hadn't hired a professional. Most of his activity—trading tokens, yield farming, earning airdrops—had been done across multiple wallets and decentralized platforms. "There's no way they'll track all this," he used to say. But now it seemed they had.

The audit notice requested detailed transaction records for two years, including all trades, income events, and wallet addresses. Panic set in. Tariq scrambled to gather data from his exchanges—some had shut down, others required days to send statements. His MetaMask transactions were a nightmare of swaps and transfers, many of which he couldn't even identify anymore. And he'd received multiple airdrops that he never valued—or reported.

He reached out to a tax attorney specializing in crypto. "You're not the first," she assured him. "But we need to reconstruct your activity, fast. They'll assume the worst unless we can prove otherwise."

For days, Tariq dove deep into block explorers, piecing together his transaction history. He used crypto tax software to import his wallet data and generate a draft Form 8949. It was eye-opening. He had over 200 taxable events in one year alone—many of which he had forgotten. Worse, his staking income had been considerable, yet he'd never declared a dollar of it.

The attorney helped him prepare a corrected return and a letter explaining his lack of knowledge, along with proof that he was now compliant. He also learned about **penalty relief options**—because he acted quickly and cooperated, the IRS was more likely to reduce the fines. But he still owed back taxes and interest. It was painful, but he was determined to fix it.

After the audit ended, Tariq made a decision: never again. He hired a crypto accountant to file quarterly estimated taxes. He began using dedicated wallets for business income and separated his long-term investments. He started saving 30% of every DeFi reward in a "tax wallet" and set calendar reminders for filing deadlines.

He also took steps to protect himself in the future. He kept organized folders with CSV exports, smart contract receipts, and valuation data for each token received. For obscure coins, he began logging CoinGecko and CoinMarketCap snapshots to verify price data. His approach went from reactive to proactive.

At a local crypto meetup, he shared his story, hoping to save others from the same fate. A young developer dismissed him: "I've never reported anything, and I've been fine."

Tariq shook his head. "So had I—until I wasn't."

The crowd grew quiet. He explained how exchanges now reported user data to the IRS, how international reporting frameworks were closing loopholes, and how even decentralized apps could be traced with the right tools. "Crypto's not invisible," he said. "It's transparent. That's the whole point."

As the industry matured, so did Tariq. He still believed in decentralization, freedom, and self-sovereignty. But he also knew that ignoring the legal side could ruin everything he had built. Compliance wasn't about selling out—it was about protecting your gains, your reputation, and your future.

Chapter 9: NFTs and Taxes: Art, Royalties, and Speculative Gains

Non-Fungible Tokens (NFTs) have added an entirely new dimension to the crypto ecosystem. From digital art and music to virtual land, gaming assets, and profile pictures, NFTs offer creators and collectors new ways to earn and engage. However, their popularity has also created tax complexities that many people still don't fully understand. The lines between personal use, investment, and business activity can become blurry—so it's essential to grasp how **NFTs are taxed**, when events are reportable, and how to track them correctly.

Let's start with the most common scenario: **buying and selling NFTs**. When you buy an NFT using cryptocurrency—such as purchasing a digital artwork with ETH—you're engaging in a taxable event. That's because you're disposing of the ETH, which is classified as property in most jurisdictions. This means you must calculate the gain or loss based on the difference between the price at which you acquired the ETH and its value at the time of the NFT purchase.

Now let's say you sell that NFT later for profit. That sale is also a taxable event. The capital gain is calculated as the difference between the NFT's sale price and its cost basis (what you paid for it, including gas fees). If you held the NFT for more than a year, you might qualify for long-term capital gains tax in some jurisdictions; otherwise, it's short-term and taxed at your regular income rate.

In countries like the U.S., **NFT gains are generally treated as capital gains**, unless you're considered a dealer or actively trading as a business. In those cases, profits may be taxed as business income, which can result in higher effective tax rates—but can also open the door to business deductions. Artists and creators who mint NFTs and sell them directly are taxed differently.

If you're an **NFT creator**, income from the initial sale is usually taxed as **ordinary income**, not capital gains. For example, if you mint and sell a digital artwork for 1 ETH, you must report the fair market value of that ETH in your local currency at the time of the sale as earned income. This applies even if the buyer paid in tokens or stablecoins.

In many jurisdictions, creators must also collect and remit **sales tax or VAT**, depending on the buyer's location. This can be difficult in decentralized environments, so creators may need to work with platforms or third-party tools to ensure compliance.

Royalties earned from **secondary market sales**—where you receive a percentage every time the NFT changes hands—are also considered income. These are usually taxed at the time they're received. Even if the tokens remain in your wallet and aren't sold for fiat, their fair market value must be reported as income on the date received.

For NFT investors, **valuation** can be tricky. Unlike cryptocurrencies with consistent market prices, NFTs are illiquid and often subjective in value. That makes determining fair market value more difficult for tax purposes. Some tax authorities may accept the last sale price or floor price on a recognized marketplace. If no recent market activity exists, estimating value becomes a gray area that requires careful documentation and conservative assumptions.

Gas fees are another important element. When minting, buying, or selling NFTs, gas fees can be significant. Fortunately, these fees are often deductible or can be added to the cost basis, reducing your taxable gain. For example, if you buy an NFT for 0.5 ETH and pay a 0.05 ETH gas fee, your total cost basis is 0.55 ETH. If you later sell the NFT for 1 ETH, your capital gain is based on 1 ETH minus 0.55 ETH, not just the purchase price.

Some NFT activity may be considered **hobby income**,

especially if done infrequently or for personal enjoyment. However, this distinction is risky, especially in cases where large amounts of money are involved. Declaring hobby income may prevent you from deducting certain expenses, so it's important to understand how your jurisdiction defines business versus hobby activity.

For tax reporting, NFT transactions must be tracked meticulously. This includes:

- Date and time of purchase or mint
- Date and time of sale or transfer
- Token ID and asset name
- Cryptocurrency used and its fair market value at the time of transaction
- Gas fees paid
- Royalties earned (including token type and value)

Several crypto tax platforms now support NFTs, but manual input is often required. You may also need to extract metadata from marketplaces like OpenSea or Rarible to verify transactions.

Finally, regulations are evolving. In the U.S., NFTs may eventually be treated similarly to **collectibles**, which could result in a higher capital gains tax rate (up to 28%). The IRS has hinted at this but has not issued formal guidance yet. Other countries may treat NFTs as intangible assets, collectibles, or even securities, depending on how they are used and marketed.

In conclusion, NFTs offer incredible potential for wealth creation, artistic expression, and innovation—but they come with real tax responsibilities. Whether you're a collector, creator, or investor, understanding the tax treatment of NFTs can help you avoid costly surprises and stay ahead in a rapidly evolving space.

How Sierra started her new business

Sierra didn't mean to start a business—she just wanted to share her art with the world. A digital illustrator from Los Angeles, she had been creating surreal landscapes and animated dreamscapes for years. But when a friend introduced her to NFTs in early 2021, everything changed. Suddenly, she was minting her artwork, listing it on OpenSea, and watching bids pour in. Within six months, she had made more money from NFTs than in her previous three years of freelancing. What she didn't realize was that the taxman had been watching too.

At first, it was thrilling. Each piece she minted sold for 0.5 to 2 ETH. Collectors raved about her work, social media followers exploded, and even a magazine reached out for an interview. But as tax season approached, her excitement turned to anxiety. She had never dealt with crypto before. She had been receiving ETH, converting some to USDC, holding others in her wallet—and never once considered the tax implications.

When she met with a tax preparer, he looked concerned. "Do you know the value of the ETH you received at the time of each sale?" he asked.

"Not really," she admitted. "I just kept track of how many ETH I got. I assumed I'd only pay taxes when I converted to dollars."

He shook his head. "You received *income* the moment someone bought your NFT. The IRS wants to know the fair market value in USD on that day—even if you didn't convert anything. And don't forget the royalties."

Sierra's jaw dropped. She hadn't even thought about the 10% royalties she was earning on resales. They were being deposited directly into her wallet from platforms like Foundation and Rarible. To her, they were bonuses—surprises. But to the government, they were *taxable income.*

They started digging through her records. Some transactions were easy to track—sales through OpenSea with timestamps and ETH values. Others, like royalties or direct transfers from private collectors, were harder to trace. And then there were the gas fees—sometimes $100 or more per mint. She had no idea those could be added to her cost basis to reduce her tax liability.

She felt overwhelmed but determined to make things right. With her accountant's help, she reconstructed her earnings: $18,500 in primary NFT sales and $4,200 in royalties. All of it would be taxed as ordinary income, not capital gains. And because she didn't have an LLC yet, she'd be paying self-employment tax on top of it.

Later that week, Sierra joined a Discord call with other NFT artists. They were sharing stories—some had formed LLCs, others were using crypto tax software to automate everything. One artist from Portugal mentioned they didn't have to pay capital gains tax at all. Another from Germany warned about the 28% collectible tax rate in the U.S. if NFTs were reclassified. The conversation was eye-opening.

One thing was clear: the IRS and other tax agencies were paying attention. A few of her peers had already received audit notices. "They're starting with high-profile wallets," someone said, "but eventually, they'll come for everyone."

Sierra made changes. She formed a single-member LLC, opened a business wallet just for NFT sales, and started tracking every transaction—date, time, value, fees. She created a system for recording royalties and began setting aside 30% of all earnings for taxes. She even began consulting with other artists, helping them navigate the confusing world of crypto tax.

The creativity was still there—the joy of making and sharing. But now, it was backed by structure, strategy, and awareness. Sierra no longer feared tax season. She had turned her NFT success into a legitimate business. And with every piece she sold, she knew not just the value of her art—but how to protect the wealth it created.

Chapter 10: Preparing for the Future: Crypto Tax Trends and Regulation Ahead

As cryptocurrencies become mainstream, governments are no longer observing from the sidelines—they are actively legislating, regulating, and enforcing. What began as a decentralized financial experiment is now on the radar of every major tax authority in the world. Investors, businesses, and even hobbyists must prepare for a future where crypto tax compliance becomes as routine and detailed as traditional finance. Understanding **where regulations are heading**, what reforms are being proposed, and how to prepare for long-term compliance is essential to navigating this evolving landscape.

In the **United States**, several developments are reshaping the crypto tax landscape. The Infrastructure Investment and Jobs Act passed in 2021 introduced broader definitions of "brokers," potentially including decentralized exchanges, wallet providers, and crypto platforms. Beginning as early as 2025, these entities will be required to issue **Form 1099-DA**, a new document tailored specifically to digital asset transactions. This means crypto users can expect direct reporting of their trades to the IRS—much like stock investors receive today from platforms like Robinhood or E*TRADE.

Another pending development is the reclassification of **NFTs and certain tokens as collectibles or securities**, which could lead to higher tax rates and stricter reporting requirements. For example, collectible assets in the U.S. can be taxed at a maximum rate of 28%, significantly higher than long-term capital gains rates. Meanwhile, discussions around crypto staking, mining, and lending are leading some regulators to consider these activities as **interest or dividend-like income**, with different tax treatment than capital gains.

Internationally, the **OECD is finalizing the Crypto-Asset Reporting Framework (CARF)**, which will require crypto platforms to share user data across jurisdictions. Much like FATCA and CRS for traditional banking, CARF aims to reduce tax evasion and increase transparency on a global scale. Countries participating in the agreement will automatically share details of crypto holdings, trades, and income events between tax authorities. If you're a digital nomad, investor, or business operating across borders, this increased transparency will limit the ability to "hide" in low-regulation countries.

In Europe, the **MiCA (Markets in Crypto-Assets) regulation** is establishing a unified legal framework across the EU. While not directly a tax law, MiCA sets the stage for stricter controls, platform accountability, and transaction documentation—meaning easier enforcement and clearer expectations for tax reporting. As these frameworks roll out, tax agencies in Europe are expected to follow with parallel rules for gains, losses, and crypto-derived income.

Looking ahead, **stablecoins and CBDCs (Central Bank Digital Currencies)** may also impact how taxes are calculated and reported. If stablecoins become fully regulated and integrated into the traditional banking system, transactions using them may trigger instant reporting or automatic tax deductions—similar to withholding tax on payroll. While this may simplify some aspects of compliance, it also reduces privacy and control.

To stay ahead of these changes, crypto participants must adopt **future-ready habits**. First, embrace proactive tax planning. This means using real-time tracking software, keeping detailed records of every crypto transaction, and categorizing activities (trading, staking, airdrops, business income) as they occur—not scrambling at year's end.

Second, diversify your tax risk. Instead of relying solely on one jurisdiction or account, explore legal strategies like forming an entity in a tax-friendly country, using multiple wallets for segmentation, or consulting international tax advisors if you have global income. With growing data sharing between countries, the only safe approach is legal compliance, backed by strategy.

Third, pay attention to **proposed legislation**, not just existing laws. Crypto tax bills are introduced regularly, and what's voluntary this year may be mandatory next year. Get on newsletters, follow updates from your tax agency, and attend webinars or conferences to stay informed.

Finally, advocate for fair crypto tax policy. As a participant in the space, your voice matters. Many tax rules being proposed today were written by people with little understanding of blockchain technology. Whether you support crypto lobbying groups, educate your representatives, or simply help your peers file accurately, you're contributing to a more balanced and transparent system.

The future of crypto taxation will be shaped by both regulators and the crypto community. Those who adapt early will not only avoid penalties—they will position themselves to thrive. Compliance will no longer be a hurdle—it will be a competitive advantage.

Now, lets go over Nico's story

Nico had always been ahead of the curve. A software engineer turned full-time DeFi strategist, he prided himself on spotting trends before they went mainstream—staking, yield farming, NFTs, DAOs. But as 2025 approached, he realized the game was shifting. Not in terms of innovation, but in regulation. The freewheeling days of crypto's early frontier were fading. The world was watching now—and governments were getting organized.

He first sensed the change when his U.S.-based exchange sent him a notification: "Starting next year, we will issue Form 1099-DA to report your digital asset transactions directly to the IRS." It felt like a punch. Nico wasn't hiding anything, but he had always enjoyed the relative privacy of crypto. Now, tax authorities were tightening the net—not just in the U.S., but globally.

At a blockchain conference in Amsterdam, he attended a panel titled *"Crypto's Regulatory Reckoning."* A Swiss lawyer explained the OECD's new Crypto-Asset Reporting Framework (CARF), where exchanges around the world would soon begin sharing user data across borders. A regulator from Germany said they were reviewing NFTs as collectibles—possibly taxing gains at up to 28%. A compliance officer from Singapore revealed that centralized platforms would soon require real-time KYC updates and tax identity verification.

"This is the new reality," the panel moderator said. "Crypto is no longer invisible. It's integrated."

Nico knew he had to evolve. He began restructuring his operation. First, he upgraded his tax software to one that integrated with DeFi protocols and NFT platforms, not just centralized exchanges. He set up alerts for taxable events in real time and started filing quarterly reports. No more last-minute spreadsheet chaos.

He also consulted a tax advisor who specialized in international compliance. They reviewed his multi-country activities—staking in Japan, DAO participation in Estonia, income from consulting projects in Argentina. They helped him draft a plan to establish clear **tax residency** in Portugal, where private crypto gains were still tax-exempt, while ensuring he wasn't inadvertently triggering dual taxation elsewhere.

The biggest change came when he reorganized his DAO contributions. Previously, he had been paid directly in tokens to his personal wallet. Now, he formed an LLC in Wyoming, funneled his earnings through the entity, and paid himself a salary. It added some paperwork—but also brought clarity, deductions, and legal separation.

When a friend asked if he was worried about losing crypto's spirit of decentralization, Nico smiled. "The mission hasn't changed," he said. "But we have to play both games now—on-chain and off-chain. If we don't adapt, the regulators will define the rules without us."

In a moment of reflection, he realized something: for years, the crypto community had feared regulation. But now, those who embraced it were the ones moving fastest. Venture capital firms demanded clean cap tables. Protocols hired CFOs. Creators tracked royalties with full audit trails. Compliance had become a competitive advantage—not a weakness.

As he looked to the future, Nico saw a new generation of builders rising—people who understood both Solidity and tax code, who knew how to code a smart contract *and* set up a legal DAO. These were the ones who would lead the next wave.

Crypto wasn't just about hiding from the old system anymore. It was about improving it—transparently, strategically, and legally. And for those willing to learn the rules while shaping the future, the opportunity was just beginning.

Turning Knowledge Into Protection and Profit

As we close this journey into the complex world of crypto taxation and regulation, one truth becomes abundantly clear: crypto is no longer a shadow economy. It's a fast-maturing financial system—one where smart individuals and businesses are using knowledge, structure, and compliance as powerful tools for long-term wealth creation.

In the beginning, crypto's appeal lay in its freedom: borderless money, peer-to-peer value, decentralized systems, and the ability to sidestep institutional friction. But freedom without accountability is a short-lived illusion. For early adopters, the lack of regulation may have felt liberating. For serious investors, entrepreneurs, and professionals, it now feels like risk.

Taxation, once seen as a threat, has become a filter—separating casual users from strategic players. Those who understand how to classify, report, and plan are preserving more of their profits. They're building scalable, legal structures, minimizing risk, and even using tax laws to their advantage through deductions, credits, and jurisdictional arbitrage.

In today's landscape, being tax-savvy is just as valuable as being tech-savvy. Those who combine the two are uniquely positioned to lead. From accurately reporting airdrops and staking rewards to forming LLCs or moving to crypto-friendly countries, informed action is the difference between fighting fires and building empires.

But this is about more than taxes—it's about mindset. Compliance isn't just paperwork; it's clarity. It's knowing that your success is sustainable. It's removing anxiety from your achievements. It's confidence that no audit, policy shift, or headline can destabilize what you've created.

As crypto moves deeper into the mainstream, regulation will not go away—it will intensify. But within that structure lies enormous opportunity. Nations will compete for crypto capital by offering better rules. Investors will flow to countries that reward innovation. Creators and businesses will thrive in jurisdictions where clarity replaces fear.

So what's next for you?

- Will you review your past activity and correct errors before it's too late?

- Will you start using tax software that tracks everything in real time?

- Will you consult professionals who understand both blockchain and tax law?
- Will you use compliance as a strategy to scale globally with confidence?

Remember, regulation doesn't kill crypto. It legitimizes it. It unlocks the doors to wider adoption, bigger investments, and long-term institutional support. Those who resist will always be reacting. Those who prepare will always be *ahead.*

Let this book be your blueprint. Come back to it often. Use it to guide your decisions, structure your systems, and educate your team. Share it with peers who still believe tax strategy is optional. It's not. It's essential.

Your crypto journey doesn't end here—it's just beginning. Now, you're not just a holder. You're a strategist. You're not just in the game. You're playing to win—and playing smart.

www.ingramcontent.com/pod-product-compliance
Lightning Source LLC
LaVergne TN
LVHW022021200926
848481LV00007B/2475